TREASURED

WRITINGS

By H. Th. Lilipaly

Translated by Andre Aki

CHRISTIAN TRINITY: A QUEST FOR TRUTH

A condensed translation from De Drie Eenheid

And Christian Trinity on a Completely Wrong Track

The Greatest Revolution in Christianity

By H. Th. Lilipaly

Translated by Andre Aki

Order this book online at www.trafford.com
or email orders@trafford.com

Most Trafford titles are also available at major online book retailers.

Printed in Victoria, BC, Canada.

ISBN: 978-1-4269-2581-8 (sc)

LIBRARY OF CONGRESS CONTROL NUMBER: 2010901599

*Our mission is to efficiently provide the world's finest, most comprehensive book publishing
service, enabling every author to experience success. To find out how to publish your book, your
way, and have it available worldwide, visit us online at www.trafford.com*

Trafford rev. 04/09/2010

 www.trafford.com

North America & international
toll-free: 1 888 232 4444 (USA & Canada)
phone: 250 383 6864 ♦ fax: 812 355 4082

CONTENTS

CHAPTER 1

A QUESTION ABOUT THE CHRISTIAN TRINITY

Is there any idea in present Christianity which could be considered as divine truth and could therefore provide us with certainty that the Trinity really exists? Taking into account all the various principles of modern Christian philosophy along with the wide range of Christian theology could we then determine the existence of the Trinity? Is there any particular idea any Biblical texts perhaps that support the idea of the true existence of the Trinity?

These are just some of the questions in the Christian religion that are haunting our thinking. Where is this certainty?

Even with in-depth thinking and the so-called objective principles, many of the statements of the Christian religion have failed to reach that point of certainty. On the contrary, modern Christianity seems to only verify weak statements or make definite statement whatsoever. Some Biblical scholars have tried made profound Biblical interpretations with a new way of thinking. They considered these to be infallible truths. But there is almost nothing from this kind of thinking that can change the orthodoxy. The analysis goes that God the Father, God the Son and God the Holy Spirit are One. But this analysis leaves many of us with a blank space in our mind. We are left without any assurance. There are no definite answers in Christianity that provide us with the confirmation of the true existence of the Trinity.

As Christians we have the right to know who God the Father is, who God the Son is and what the Holy Spirit is. With the many different opinions and views in Christianity it is very difficult to validate the existence of the Trinity. We take it for granted what has been constituted by the Church the dogmatic concept regarding the existence of God the Father, the Son and the Holy Spirit. Other opinion even goes further declaring the philosophy of the Triune God, the Three in One and the One in Three God. These are based on various Biblical interpretations and several clerical convictions that refer to different canonical sources. But all these theological confusions do not produce certainty about the reality of the actual existence of God in the Trinity. Why not? Because no matter how intellectual we have become we are still mortals with limited mortal thinking, no matter how intellectually we have become. We can never enter the threshold of the Divine! We see the aimless struggling of the theologians and philosophers as signs of their confusion and doubts.

Many learned Christians discuss the Trinity concept subjectively and objectively with compulsive meditations and yet they come up with different ideas and dogmatic determinations. Where then might we obtain convincing truth about the Threefold Unity? Where might we find a certain degree of certainty and be inspired by the principles of a high standard of Christian thinking?

This book is a special instruction of GOD the Father and the Son of God - Jesus Christ who came to me and whom I have received at the foot of the CROSS of Golgotha-Calvary to confirm the absolute answer to the question.

Allow me also to explain that the revelations and divine messages which I have received are very difficult for the human mind to accept. These messages may not be accepted by the reader, but my task and the instruction I have received from my Lord Jesus Christ is to pass it on to the world in a book form. Things which are placed in the Light of the Cross and the Resurrection of Christ are difficult to understand and are in general determined by our relationship with Christ and to the principles of human ability.

Throughout the ages Christian philosophers and theologians have tried to present to us the truth of the Trinity through dogmatic formulas and doctrines, though, speculations, through research and contemplations of the Bible. But they have never been able to create a definite faith, an intrinsic truth. Therefore let us give ourselves the chance to accept the principles of the reality of the mystery of GOD in the Light of the CROSS of Christ. The Cross will lead us to discover the secret of the divine Truth, its wisdom and certainty. Every Christian should be able to anticipate the truth of God. If we let the Cross of Christ dominate our Christian thinking, then we will meet the Truth of GOD.

*see some of my earlier books: Experiences with God and His Messengers,Exposition Press,Inc.New-York,1980,Gott findet man nur irn Kreuz Christi ,1997 by R.G. Fischer Verlag, Frankfurt/Main)

CHAPTER II

GOD THE FATHER

*The Christian problem - God the Father in Christianity -
the developing reality and established views.*

The question concerning God the Father prevalent in the Christian religion
requires a response. Christian thinking demands certainty and truth. Several
arguments among believers have developed to such a degree that it has left
many of us in a position difficult to accept certain religious matters. Is there
a GOD and does this GOD really exists? Who is GOD and how could
we accurately say what HE is like? We have seen multitudes of different
arguments about GOD in Christianity that left us in a limbo. On the other
hand many efforts by the church have been implemented to provide the
congregation with some proof of the existence of a GOD like in many
other religions. This GOD that is GOD the Father is proven with certain
theological and many biblical terms, and we all are expected to willingly
accept the findings that have been regulated by the church and demand
that this belief not be rejected or refute. But neither Christianity nor the
Christians are able to grasp the truth of the existence of GOD the Father
with all of our existing theologies and the varieties of our bibles! Books,
magazines, newspapers are full of criticism and demand proof! The question
of GOD the Father has started a revolution in our minds, because of the
many challenging viewpoints the world over. The contrasts in Christianity
between various Christian groups have created tensions. We observe the
developments of new ideas put forth by many theologians and Christian

philosophers based on certain view points and an in-depth study of the bible through out the ages. Myriads of doctrines and Christian concepts have become conglomerate of facts based on biblical texts and ideas become analyzable biblical expositions. Yet the profound theologians are unable to reveal any new information except the dogmas which have been adopted as truths.

And we have to come to conclusion that in our flight of fancy or illusion we have accepted these doctrines as being the infallible truth and the direct message from GOD via the bible without realizing that have never been so. GOD the Father has not been speaking to us through these texts in the bible- but it has been our own ideas which have created an illusion, a fantasy, which we have accepted in its entirety as divine truth!

Is there a GOD- God the Father? Does this God, GOD the Father indeed exist and if HE does WHO is this GOD? How can we answer these questions with certainty and make it realistic? I really hope that there is something in our minds which guide us to make the right conclusions answering the above questions. All religions in the world admit and confess that there is a GOD, and in Christianity we call HIM, GOD the Father- GOD the Father of Jesus Christ. Generally Christians have accepted the existence of GOD the Father and put HIM in a special position. We have verified this position through a variety of biblical texts, which we believe are spiritually inspired or confirmed by a revelation from GOD. However we should not easily jump to the conclusion as if all biblical texts as infallible and exempted from errors.

After years long struggle in spirit at the foot of the CROSS of CHRIST here is the message that I have to convey to the world directly from GOD the Father and JESUS CHRIST that the Truth of the existence of GOD the Father and HIS divine Character can only be discovered in the Light of the CROSS in the context of His Resurrection. With an indepth understanding of the CROSS of CHRIST we should be able to recognize the spiritual character of the existence of GOD and be directed to the Truth about GOD the Father and enable us to spiritually discern in our mind that this GOD the Father is. The CROSS of CHRIST contains all the elements of divine Truth in terms of doctrine or impressions of GOD the Father. Hence we accept that there is a GOD- God the Father and indeed without a doubt GOD exists! Consequently our next question remains: Who is this God the Father?

Through the CROSS came the ultimate reply that GOD God the Father-is the Holy Father of JESUS CHRIST. GOD GOD the Father- has no beginning and no end. Nobody, no living soul no matter what power of perception and reasoning is no mortal would he able to unravel the mystery and Arcanum of God the Father.

These are things that belong to the highest form of divinity, matters unattainable by the human mind no matter what form of rationality we may employ. GOD- God the Father- is the Father of JESUS CHRIST, He is the Creator and Supreme Being of the world, the universe, and the firmament and everything divine in the entire creation. GOD- God the Father is the Almighty, the CREATOR of all things. Everything that lives and breaths is because of God the Father, the Original, the Infinite, the Eternal and Omnipotent. Everything that has been developed in every area of the world, every power or form of life in the whole creation, has been because of God the Father. We will only be able to see and understand this thought through the Cross of Christ in the Light of the Resurrection. This should be an underlying part of our faith.

When we speak of God the Father as the Absolute and Creator of all things we should immediately cast our mind to the Cross of Christ in relationship to the Resurrection as opposed to the view that reject to accept the Cross of Christ as the only medium leading to understand the creation, the work of God the Father. I fully understand that this view is contradictory to the teachings of the orthodoxy, but I like to stress with deep conviction that we will only comprehend the significance of God's work of creation through the deepest understanding of the CROSS of CHRIST.

All Christian ideas and principles regarding God- the Creator of all things need to be viewed through the CROSS in the Light of the Resurrection as the only answer of all our questions.

We might try to interpret the meaning of GOD the Father thru religious teachings and refer to the various biblical texts available but those are only words for us to contemplate but it will never give us the very truth to enlighten our minds.

GOD is God the Father, and there is only One God and no other God who is not GOD the Father of Jesus Christ! Let's stretched it a little bit further. God is God the Father and His Son is JESUS CHRIST. There is prominently One God and no other God. He is the Supreme Being, the only One GOD Who creates. I state this fact that undoubtedly God creates only thru His Son Jesus Christ.

God is the Creator and CHRIST is the Direct Creator of every object in the world that we may come across, whatever it might be.

But let us not, I repeat let's not split or divide GOD into God the Father and God the Son. CHRIST is the Son of GOD and NOT God the Son. The idea of God the Son as mentioned in the Trinity dogma has lead us totally in a wrong direction and has misguided us to follow an un-trustworthy and inaccurate course. This line of thinking has made many of our theologians look like fools and many others as simpletons.

Concepts regarding the three manifestation of God in the Trinity namely God the Father, God the Son and God the Holy Ghost have been explained and reinforced by Christian philosophers and theologians thru the ages should be denied and immediately corrected. Because there is only preeminently One GOD ... GOD the Father- and CHRIST His Son. God the Father and Christ and the Holy Ghost are not Gods or Gods in ONE GOD.

Correspondingly although Christianity clearly states to the contrary, there is not God the Son in the Trinity, but just CHRIST - the Son of God. I repeat again there is no God the Son and no God the Holy Ghost, just JESUS CHRIST the SON of God and the Holy Ghost which is the divine authority of God the Father operating in this world.

There is an absolute nebulousness and a fundamental confusion regarding the Trinity concept. We should not and never accept the wrong interpretation of the three forms and characters of God as laid down in the Trinity. It is improper, inappropriate, unsuitable within any frame of thinking no matter how professionally it may seem based on the biblical teachings! Christianity has created a wrong understanding and awareness and shape of God in the Trinity concept and millions members and congregations have accepted without even thinking. Anything as declared in the Trinity dogma has been agreed and confessed by Christianity and the church is delusive and unreal. It creates confusion in the mind and we hardly can distinguish the things that we should accept as truth. Let me again repeat my statement: there is only one God- God the Father ... the Father of Jesus Christ. This Almighty GOD informs us of His wish that we meet with Him only thru His Son: JESUS CHRIST and not thru any other religion, theism, belief or faith in the world. God wants us to come into His presence through His only begotten Son Jesus Christ, the Crucified and Resurrected Christ of Golgotha/Calvary

I again reaffirm the essence of the message I received directly from God and Christ, that there is solely only ONE GOD- the only God- and no other God than the GOD of Jesus Christ, the Father of Jesus Christ. CHRIST and likewise the Holy Ghost are not Gods as Christianity and the church have proclaimed and I hereby denounce its existence and also reject the Triune or Trinity theology. Historically Christian philosophers and theologians have provided the basis of the formation by combining a variety of biblical texts and doctrines and believing them to be the only true revelations of God and Christ. And because of this peculiarity we have a lot of misrepresentation and distortion on our hands. There are a large number of religions in the world. Each one has the faith and belief that there is a God and that this God really exists in whatever condition or place they would suppose to have Him. The existence of God is the divine proof of the living God- the God of Christ- God the Father God the Father of Christ. When we exchange ideas about God, we fail to comprehend in our conscious mind that God the Father - the God of Christ is included in that terminology. It should be the basis of our contemplations. We used to assign many names to God; however, this God has only ONE NAME He is God the Father- the God of CHRIST-God the Father of Christ. This is an established principle and a divine fact and must be eagerly received by every Christian and any other member of any religious order in the world who has religious convictions and who holds as truth that there is actually a GOD, that this God really exist- and that He is not a figment of the imagination.

GOD the Creator is the living God of Christ. God does exist and is not just something that has been created by religion to be estimated as a god- an object for divine mediation.

Finally, every teaching that divides God into three divine beings as in the Trinity dogma is a complete depravity of the true significance of GOD. He is God the Father- God the Father of CHRIST -the God of Jesus Christ.

Finally God-God the Father- is the Father of Christ, -and Christ being the direct creator of all things. As we mentioned that although God the Father is the Creator of all things, yet He did not perform the entire creation directly, but created it through CHRIST. We will better understand this proposition if we perceived it through the CROSS of Christ. Through the heart of the Cross and the Resurrection of Christ will we be able to acquire knowledge of the divine workings of God the Father that will stimulate our thinking and develop our mind. We will obtain confidence and the fullness of faith by realizing the truth and purpose of the divine CROSS of CHRIST, in the Light of the Resurrection. The GOD- GOD the Father- as HE is referred in this chapter is the Father of CHRIST, He is the Lord and the Almighty, the Supreme Being and the Absolute, the Original and the Father, the Author and Creator of all things, the King of Kings and the Lord of Lords, the Infinite and the Eternal, the All- Powerful- the Omnipotent, the All Wise and the All-knowing- the Omniscient.

The explanation I have presented in this chapter hopefully will present you the answers to the questions about the existence of God the Father and help you realize who this God is.

CHAPTER III

GOD THE SON

Questions about the Trinity - The mystery of Christ - Questions about God the Son - The bridgeless gap in the human mind.

The questions which have developed in Christianity regarding CHRIST (God the Son as He is referred to in the Trinity) have dominated the thoughts of many Christians desiring to get a firm grip on the facts of what they believe in. Too many of these are serious matters and have endeavored to find reliable conclusions thru exhaustive analysis of various biblical texts, thinking that in this way they would find greater understanding of the facts regarding the problem of JESUS CHRIST or God the Son as He is referred to in the Trinity dogma.

The dominant questions right now are: Who is CHRIST and what is His divine character as the Son of God? What is His place and relationship to this Trinity theology in which He took the place as God the Son? I explained in chapter II of this book that GOD is the Father of JESUS CHRIST and His name is God the Father, and accept this reality as absolute Truth without any doubt.

Christ- Jesus Christ- has been ascribed to be the Son of God- God's Son. However we should be able to clearly distinguish, knowing that Christ is the Son of God, we cannot quote the Trinity in our confession and call Christ God the Son. Reason: because there are not two Gods, there is only One God, GOD the Father- the Father of Jesus Christ. In this particular case we should call Jesus Christ-God's Son- the Son of God and NOT

God the Son. It is incorrect to say God the Son. This is in accordance to the divine message I received from God and Christ that GOD- God the Father- is the only ONE GOD and that CHRIST JESUS is the only ONE Son of God, which is completely not in line with the Trinity of the church! I strongly suggest that Christianity should change its fundamental theology and basic doctrine! This differing opinion of Christians and Christian theologians on the concept of the Trinity need to be corrected and Christianity has to come to grips with it. At the same time the churches should solve the problems as spiritual justification. And if needed be revise their positions. It is not only a philosophical and theological problem with the churches but more so the theological truth. To achieve a better degree of understanding about the above questions we should take our mind back to Golgotha/Calvary concentrating fully on the Cross of Christ, God's Son, and seeing Christ entirely as the living object of our life. Only thru this spiritual exercise by fully concentrating on the CROSS at Calvary/Golgotha and deeply entering into the knowledge of the Cross will we be able to understand who CHRIST is in this particular relationship. Because the existence of CHRIST, and our belief in HIM can only be realized at the CROSS. Similarly the answer to the question as who CHRIST is can only be determined at the CROSS of Golgotha. How we dealt with this struggle illustrate our genuine endeavors for the truth. The CROSS, within the frame of the Resurrection is the genuine answer and solution to the problem of who Christ is and likewise to that of whether Christ really exists! According to the scriptures Christians and theologians corroborated that Christ really exist. And the bible has been referred as the only medium thru which God could speak to us. It is so because it has to be so! Really?

I am concerned that Christianity has become just theology and dogmatic faith. I wonder whether it is really God God the Father- who is speaking to us thru the biblical texts in the bible. We need a change in our spiritual climate and a change in the religious crisis of today. I am very critical of the Christian theological language and the dogmatic concepts that in many cases oversimplify the things that pertain to the area of the divine. We should dare to denounce the distorted relations as well as its fragmentations. It is worth pausing to reflect the immense danger of misinterpreting and misjudge the biblical texts. Since the objective of reading the bible is a kind of philosophy of revelation a revelation from God we then caricaturize that our religious intellect when reading the bible has reached the threshold of the divine. "God says it, because the bible says it." And nothing could be more wrong than this suggestion. Let us leave the mysteries of God to God and Christ themselves. There is no foundation for us to become Gods translators! We are at war with our own church, our own theologians, and our own preachers. Christianity has been guilty for many reasons: unspeakable treatment and exploitation of native populations, the wars of greed and colonization, racial supremacy, the wars of religion etc. But most of all let us not alienate the gospel of Jesus Christ- His crucifixion, His Cross, His death, with esoteric languages and spoil the true meaning of His Finished Work, by using poor translations, corrupt texts, misinterpretations, and doctrinal misunderstandings. We must get back to the essence of Christianity. not by waging war against the church but looking for the truth and not accepting anything what the Church said is true but by objectively looking at the dogmas in the light of the Cross; Christianity relates in the Trinity dogma that Christ is the Son of Man, but we need to be very cautious in interpreting this. Let us not try as humans interpret things that belong to the area of the divine. There are matters that will remain a mystery of GOD and CHRIST alone, completely beyond our power of understanding, impermeable by our human mind. Considering the fact that Christ is the Son of God let us not crack our brain trying to know as to what kind of Man Christ is. Let us leave this kind of matters to God and Christ alone! I repeat CHRIST, Jesus Christ, the Messiah, the Anointed One, the Savior and Redeemer is the Son of God, and I believe that we hopefully will understand all these if we one day may see God and Christ. Let's therefore be very cautious using the term Christ the Son of Man. Due to the fact the very being, entity, subsistence and nature of Christ is identical, being the very same as of God the Father, His Father.

Let's conclude in the final judgment that Christ is the Son of God, in His intimate role as the Almighty and Supreme Being, The Direct Absolute and The First Cause, The Direct Infinite and The Direct Eternal, The Direct Omniscient and The Direct Omnipotent, The direct All-wise and The Direct All-merciful-in short, CHRIST is The Direct Creator of all things.

The mystery of CHRIST- the SON of GOD, and CHRIST - the Son of Man- can only be understood and perceived at Golgotha at the foot of the CROSS of Christ. Through the CROSS of Christ we will be able to comprehend the reality of the Truth of God and Christ! Evidence of this is a characteristic private personal experience, unable to be epitomized in words. You have to encounter and experience this yourself. You have to concentrate all your meditation and consciousness on the Cross of Christ. You have to perceive the Crucified Christ in the Light of His Resurrection, coming down in your life, and God and Christ will fill you with their divine might and omnipotence. The entire power and force of your thinking will be seized and clutched in the hands of this divine power. You would then behold the facts and recognize the reality of the Truth of God and Christ. Imperatively you have to kneel down at the foot of the Cross of Christ, fixing your minds eyes completely on the Crucified Christ, while you close your eyes concentrate entirely on the CROSS of Christ, perceiving the blood of Christ pouring out of His wounds. You have to envision the suffering and dying Christ on the Cross of Golgotha as it happened, then you would be able to describe the reality and witness the Truth of God the Father and Christ, the Son of God. In this particular way you hopefully would be able to understand the reference of Christ the Son of Man.

God the Father, and Christ -the Son of God themselves will reveal to you thru the revelation of the Cross and Resurrection of Christ, since these matters are not things which can be depicted in words or easily understood by mortal minds. We could mention our contiguity with God and Christ at the foot of the CROSS of Golgotha as something decidedly divine, an elucidatory contact, insolvable by any human statement or declaration, something superhuman, celestial and godlike- something that sustains all conditions, endures as the extreme of all mysteries. I strongly belief that this divine disclosure will be clearer to us when we have left this world and are there close to God the Father and Christ, the Son of God. If we really wish to know the existence of God and Christ and be convinced as who this infallible God and His Son are then without any doubt I must ask you and invite you to come to the covered with blood holy Cross of Calvary, and concentrate completely on the Crucified Christ- the Son of God, the Son of Man and you definitely will obtain the immense and wonderful answer, because the CROSS of Christ in the Light of the Resurrection is the only response and rebuttal to all questions and doubtful problems. With this chapter I hereby clarify that I reject and refuse to accept the dogma and concept of the Trinity that has been established by the church throughout the ages! May the explanation of this chapter bring us all closer into communion with God and His Son Jesus Christ. It is by no means a new expression in Christianity but a true "approach" to find the true living GOD and His Son Jesus Christ

Chapter IV

God the Holy Spirit

God the Holy Ghost, God the Holy Spirit, in the Trinity Dogma, The Christian Analysis-Right or Wrong?

The idea that the Holy Ghost or Holy Spirit is God, as mentioned in the Christian dogma of the Trinity, is problematic. What are the basic assumptions of this dogma? Was it based on Biblical texts and developed as a religious reflection? For centuries, the church has been preaching the Holy Ghost as God, which has resulted in doubts and confusions in Christian communities and has left so many churches empty. Christianity should pay serious attention to this phenomenon, particularly within the young generation, or become a victim of its own fabrications. This fable of God the Holy Ghost is a product of the church and has been promulgated by it to maintain its grip on Christian society.

We should dare to challenge the church and Christianity in general and remind them that they are on the wrong track. If we know for sure that something is false and untrue in Christianity, we should not fear to be unpopular. We should be prepared for a decline of faith and an irretrievable fall in Christianity. Because we never look at the CROSS when interpreting the Bible, we are not controlled by consistent reasoning. How can we ask people to believe in the Trinity (three gods) while the thesis makes no sense at all?

I believe that we should fill in the gaps and fractures in Christianity with the knowledge of the Cross of the Son of God, who died at Calvary.

Christianity has been deflected from its original mission. It seems to have reached the end of its journey. Based on the divine message which I have received from God and Christ, I must inform you and the world that the Holy Ghost, or Holy Spirit, is not, I repeat,-is not God. And hereby I reject the concept and dogma of the Trinity.

What was the fundamental mistake of this theology?

What were the Biblical statements used to support the Trinity? If there are none, Who or What, then, is the Holy Spirit or Holy Ghost? The question now calls for an answer, a firm and convincing answer. The concept of GOD the Father is deeply embedded in Christianity. We hear every Christian pray in the churches, "Our Father Who is in heaven," but to feel the real presence of the Holy Spirit, we must reach that level of faith and knowledge of the Cross that only a few can reach in the Light of the CROSS and the Power of Christ's Resurrection.

And the Holy Ghost? The Holy Ghost or Holy Spirit is the heavenly and supreme Power of God and Christ that is effectively working in this world and in the entire universe. By means of this divine ascendancy, God and Christ in heaven effectively constitute Their Divine Will and work in accordance with Their Purpose and wishes, carrying out what has been designed and sealed in Their Divine Plan. God and Christ act through this power that we call the Holy Spirit or Holy Ghost. As a result of this Holy Spirit or Holy Ghost, man is helped to recognize the difference between good and evil and everything associated with justice, mercy, and loving-kindness,

Eliminate the above-mentioned concept, remove the concept of rationality, eliminate the concept of a universal creation of a family with God as a Father, and we will have an utterly uninteresting, lame, and lifeless proposition. The encounter between the Creator and man, in whatever way one likes to explain it, presents us with the insight that there is a Living and Loving Creator. The actual encounter with an actual divine revelation can only be understood if man stands in front of the Cross of the direct Creator, Without the Holy Spirit, or Holy Ghost, we would never be able to perceive the origin or nature of what is good. Similarly, without the Holy Spirit, we would never have the power to recognize the distinct characteristics of good and evil. As a consequence of the Holy Spirit's work, we will be able to enter into a spiritual communion with God and Christ. The Holy Spirit also assists us in recognizing the divine things from God and Christ, matters which ye could determine as good. It has taken centuries for the Christian mind to realize the full extent of good and evil. I realize that this book is not the appropriate forum in which to discuss at length the language of good and evil, yet I base my opinion on my personal experiences at the foot of the CROSS of Christ and my vision of the real. In sum, when we receive ideas which are good, they come from God and Christ, whereas the ideas which are evil come from the devil. This is an interpretation influenced by Christian theology (Romans 2: 14) and modern political theory.

Particularly during the early decades of the Christian faith, Christians were inclined to expect much guidance from God and Christ. This guidance was the object of serious religious contemplation of the signs of God's presence and those of Christ through the Holy Spirit. The doctrine of the Holy Spirit is intrinsically dependent on the transcendent principle, the idea of God's and Christ's immanent presence(Colossians 1:16), but only if the Christian can envision himself surrendering at the feet of the CROSS of His Master and God. When we read the Bible and attempt to understand the Biblical texts, which is not as easy as we think, we tell our mind to come to the truth of God and Christ and hope and pray that the Holy Spirit will work in us. Thus we attempt to express the mystery of God and Christ and trust for a genuine Christian interpretation. Nonetheless, interpretation may or may not be dubious, or even moot. So how do we know the actual truth that the Holy Spirit is working through us? All things may come to pass through your degree of faith, the grade of your faith in Christ's Finished Work and in God. But our personal spiritual intentions may go in the opposite direction.

Once again, Christians may come to trust their good impulses and pay attention to the subtler feelings and emotions of their soul because all principles, actions, activities, and thoughts of what is truly good come from God and Christ through the Holy Spirit. What we read in the Bible and hear in the churches should be the guiding principles for a contemplative life if they proceed through the Holy Spirit. There is no way we can understand any truth without them. The achievements of science and technology, the cryptic Christian mysteries, which have been revealed, are expressions of the working power of the Holy Spirit.

For ages, Christian theologians and the Church have created and falsely claimed that the Holy Ghost or Holy Spirit is the third god in the Trinity. What is the initial impulse of this mentality? That Christianity has attempted a reunion with the Greek mythology or Hinduism? I hope not. We all have a tremendously serious accountability to HIM who gave His life at the CROSS at Calvary.

In the final part of this chapter, I shall try respond to the religious predicament that theologians and the church have failed to explain. During my sixty-five years of Christian life as preacher, I have been struggling with the ambiguity inherent in the term Trinity. My mental and spiritual lives seemed at times go their own ways until September 15, 1946, and

January19, 1947, when I had my encounters with my Lord and Savior Jesus Christ. These encounters are the reason for the tone and orientation of my personal spirituality. Increasingly separated from systematic Protestant theology, my spiritual life was forced to coin a language of its own.

My mental and spiritual lives go their own ways. Through my struggle with the Truth of GOD the Father and Jesus Christ the Son of GOD at the foot of the CROSS of Calvary, I was supernaturally instructed to pass on the divine message stated in the previous chapter. 1 realize that it will come as a surprise to readers, but who are we, by any authority, to deny, to discern the true from the false, the good from the evil, the just from the unjust?

I ask you to read my books with an open mind in the Light of the CROSS. May CHRIST Himself remove the major roadblocks that have hinder you from finding the true revelation of GOD the Father and CHRIST the Son of GOD.

*see some of my earlier books: Experiences with God and His messengers. Exposition Press, Inc. New York, 1980. Gott findet nur irn Kreuz Christi, 1997 by Fischer Verlag. Frankfurtl Main

CHAPTER V

GOD'S WORD

*The Holy Bible, God's Word, Preaching Reality, Fallacies
and Clerical Misjudgment*

Is the Holy Bible really God's Word? With translations of the Bible into so
many languages and so many different interpretations of the same texts, we
can seriously inquire whether the Bible is indeed God's Word. If it is, then
why are some parts left out and expelled?

In an attempt to answer the first question, some influential theologians
and many preachers are advocating concepts of God and the Bible that are
radically different from what is described in the scriptures of Christianity,
Judaism, and Islam. Many feel that it is impossible to take a stand on religion,
and many more feel like they are walking in the dark and see no light. There
are too many questions in Christianity that are related to the Holy Bible.
To understand the Bible, it is not sufficient to know the historical facts.
One must have an encounter with the Truth. For many, to read the Bible
means to search for God, but interpreting the message has created many
denominations, and only God knows what proliferation of churches, with
their enormous variety in liturgy, doctrines, and practices. How many times
do we hear the preacher or pastor in his opening passage quoting from the
prophets, "For thus said the Lord that created the heavens," etc. etc., and the
result is deeply stirring. The congregation accepts the preacher's words as if
they have just heard God's Own Word. Although we realize that the verses

of the Bible can be interpreted metaphorically as well as allegorically, we have allowed ourselves to be swept up by this kind of "orthodoxy."

A true Christian believer may not follow the path of this kind of orthodoxy. God is only to be found in the CROSS of His Son Jesus Christ at Calvary in the Light of His Resurrection. You can see it with the eyes of your faith when you kneel down at the foot of the CROSS of the Redeemer. If you read your Bible, read it in the Light of the CROSS and the Resurrection of CHRIST, and you will find the truth of God's Word, and hear God and Christ speaking to you. If we master that faith where we can see ourselves at the foot of the CROSS of Christ and focus our vision only on the Crucified Son of God, I promise you that you will experience that emotion so passionate that is impossible for the human tongue to explain the power of the Holy Spirit. All that is required is a complete surrender at the foot of the CROSS of Christ. But it is a continuing spiritual struggle for our soul because outside of the periphery of the CROSS, we are lost.

So let us read the Bible in the Light of the CROSS so that it becomes a true revelation from God and Christ. Without Christ's Cross and His Resurrection, the Bible is only a book written by human beings. But place it in the Light of the Cross, and you will experience the working of the power of the Holy Ghost through the Cross. Only through this divine direction will we hear Gods word in the Bible.

How often do we forget that the father of lies, the devil, always likes to interfere in our journey to serve God? Lucifer lives among us. We underestimate the devil's power. He sends his followers to attend churches to make sure that the congregations do not receive the truth. When we as preacher or priest stand in the pulpit, I presume that the believing congregation (our parishioners) expects that God and Christ will speak to them through us. This lifts the dimension of Biblical theology up some notches. We follow the traditional religious tradition and come to believe that God is with us. It could hardly be otherwise, given the theology and doctrine of God. I believe that Christianity has "demoralized" its congregations, for whatever reason, in this way.

The concept of "God with us" in this perspective is misleading and dangerous. It is more accurate to say that God is to be found only at the CROSS of Christ His Son.

I have to repeat myself. The divine message I received from Christ and must convey to the world is that through the sermon we must be able to see with the eyes of our soul the Crucified and Resurrected CHRIST. Only then can we convincingly say that God and Christ speak through our sermons. As I said earlier, because of the words, "Thus saith the Lord," a Biblical tradition is sometimes lifted out of the context of the Bible and is, at the same time, influenced by "romanticism." A thoroughly understanding of the relationship of GOD the Father and Christ the Son and the Holy Ghost is essential. In the dimension of relation of GOD the-Father, Christ the Son of God, and the Holy Ghost, we must confess that what needs to be changed in Christianity in its belief system. Our civilization and church orthodoxy, perhaps inevitably, perhaps unknowingly, have resulted in a threat to mankind, particularly to Christian believers. We must seek to change the very tradition of the dogma of the Christian Trinity. For me and some other Christians, this divine mandate holds a serious directive: Christianity is presently in a crisis. We are obligated to examine our past critically with the hope of repentance at the foot of the CROSS. Then we must go out into this world in crisis to reshape our belief system in GOD the Father, CHRIST Jesus the SON, and the Holy Ghost.

As a final point in this chapter before we end this discussion of God's Word and the application of the Holy Scripture, allow me to recapitulate my argument of this aspect of the discussion.

1. When we speak of the Holy Scripture as God's Word, the essential and main character should be CHRIST and Christ alone, His CROSS, and His Resurrection. Without the above elements, there is no God's Word.

2. When we preach, our concept and thought should be based on Christ, His Cross, and His Resurrection. We should perceive Christ, His Cross and His Resurrection in our mind and soul. Let the working power of the Holy Ghost work through us so that our eyes of faith can see Him bleeding on the Cross for us, for the entire congregation, as the quintessence of His Finished Work at Calvary. This dimension of relationship with God and Christ can only be linked if we kneel down at the foot of the Cross and at His Pierced Feet ask Him to enter into our soul and mind (and that of our congregation) and ask the power of the Holy Ghost to work in us so that the congregation can feel that God and Christ are speaking to them.

We must break the chain of orthodoxy, a lukewarm Christianity, and hear the voice of the Crucified One, the voice of God through the Cross and Resurrection, and we must allow our tears of regret and repentance to flow during our prayers so that they will be picked up and stored in the heavenly basins.

3. The potency and power of God's Word- through the Holy Scripture is located in the heart of the CROSS of CHRIST. If we are honest, this revelation of the truth of God and Christ will come to us and we will accept this truth as a living reality in our life.

4. Yet it is necessary to be wary that we should and must stay with this divine truth and not run from the facts that drive us to the certainty of faith. We must not fall back into our religious heresy.

We know if we are honest, that we should not succumb to any influence of human principles, ideas, and interpretations that keep us away from the truth. Remember, Christianity is not Christ. Religion is not God. But Christianity and religion are related to Christ and God.

In summary, may the Light of the Crucified CHRIST come to us so that we might hear the Voices of God and Christ speaking to us through the Bible, the Holy Scripture, so that we know it is God Who is speaking to us through the working of the Holy Spirit.

In conclusion on these reflections on the Bible, God's Word, and reality I think it is because we are fearful of correcting of what is wrong in Christianity. To correct what is wrong is to allow the Crucified Christ to come to us when we kneel at His Pierced Feet at the Cross so that we can hear God and Christ speaking to us through the Holy Bible and through the working of the Holy Spirit. But a preliminary step we must take, in addition to constant and regular prayer at the foot of the CROSS, is to believe in His Finished Work at Calvary. CHRIST has a judgment waiting, believe it or not, for those who intentionally neglect to mention His Finished Work in their sermons and other works.

And when we preach, let us always set our mind to the CROSS of CHRIST at Golgotha so that we may see the truth of the revelation of God and CHRIST operating through the Bible. May our sermons shed light to the Light of the Cross so that our souls will not get lost in the darkness of this world. May the very heart of the CROSS, of God and Christ, speak through our sermons to our congregations. I conclude this chapter with a wish and prayer that Christians all over the world realize that something is wrong with Christianity today and that we should be seriously change our patterns of thought before it is too late.

CHAPTER VI

GOD'S REVELATION

God's Revelation. Critical Problems in
Our Christian Thinking

The problems with revelations from God are complex in their ramifications. A revelation is and must inevitably be a personal experience. Revelations from God require some philosophical inquiries. A deep, ethical, religious analysis will take us to the concept of GOD, holiness, salvation, and eternal life.

It is impossible in this short undertaking to analyze these complex subjects. The various natures of our upbringing, education, and viewpoint have created different viewpoints in us. For the present purpose, however, this difference does not matter. There will probably (and possibly) never be a universally accepted, standard definition for revelation. I will speak of my personal experience and my honest interpretation of what I must do. But the message and revelation I received from GOD and CHRIST can only be understood in the Light of the CROSS if we kneel down at the foot of the CROSS at Calvary/Golgotha in the heart of His Resurrection.

Our next obligation, then, is to take the appropriate approach to seek a philosophical understanding of what revelation is. My Christian faith is philosophically elaborated through a long, personal struggle of Christian thought at the foot of the Cross of the Crucified CHRIST.

In the Old Testament, prophets such Isaiah, Jeremiah, and others are believed to have received revelations from God, whereas the letters of Paul and John are categorized as revelations from Christ. The revelations in the

New Testament are said to be "different" from the revelations and messages in the Old- Testament. The later visions, messages, and revelations are more "personal." From this spiritual point of view, the answer to the above question depends on the way we define "revelation." Revelations belong to the internal life of faith of a person; they are not means to evangelize to the world.

The central question now is this: What is the basis for believing that these revelations exist? It is sometimes not possible to establish the existence of a revelation by rational argument. Christians from different churches and different theologians have stressed revelations by rationalism, by reasoning, others by empiricism. This is true in religion as in many other fields. If God exists, this is not an idea, but a reality. Therefore to be known by us, HE will have to manifest Himself in some way to us. But our senses can delude us. In my personal experience, we oftentimes underestimate Lucifer, the devil, who not only can deceive us but also can tamper with our minds. In this instance, our level of faith is determinative. What are your grounds to belief in God? In my case, to venture and discover God and CHRIST in my life is by total surrender at the foot of the CROSS.

There are many explanations in Christianity of revelation based on the writings of distinguished philosophers and authors based on the Bible. These are complex in their structure and development. The authors express their opinions about the truth of the revelation in accordance with the intellectually deep study of the Bible, yet we only arrive at a stage of religious philosophizing and never meet the living God, because GOD is only to be found in the CROSS of CHRIST His Son.

This is, to me, the most important element for Christianity because it involves being engaged in the spiritual struggle at the foot of the Cross. The language of the Cross deals with salvation, eternal life, sacrifice, guilt, despair, the soul, and death.

The message for every Christian-believer that I must reveal is that the true revelation of God and Christ can only be observed in the Light of the Cross of Christ and in the very heart of His Resurrection. Only at the foot of the CROSS will the revelation become the truth and elucidate who God is and who Christ is and what the Holy Spirit is. Christians should not try to find God in the Bible. He is not there. God and Christ are not dependent on the Bible. God and Christ are not created. They are eternal, without beginning and without end. Building upon this immoveable characteristic of certainty, our Christian belief system should be able arrive at the truth of the revelation through the Cross.

The CROSS should be the primary consideration of our Christian argument to obtain valid reasoning because the revelation of God as represented in the CROSS of CHRIST takes us to a higher level of faith. Only in the CROSS of Christ will God manifest Himself to us human beings. This disclosure is a revelation, and for us it is faith. This view is a communication of the truth and consent as Pascal★ expresses it with great clarity:

It was not then right that HE should appear in a manner manifestly divine and completely capable of convincing all men; but it was also not right that HE should come in so hidden a manner that HE could not be known by those who should sincerely seek HIM. HE has willed to make HIMSELF quite recognizable by those; and thus, willing to appear openly to those who seek HIM with all their heart, and to be hidden from those who flee from HIM with all their heart, HE so regulates the knowledge of HIMSELF that HE has given signs of HIMSELF, visible to those who seek HIM, and not to those who seek HIM not. There is enough light for those who only desire to see, and enough obscurity for those who have a contrary disposition.

In closing, allow me to remind readers of the purpose of this brochure. I have written about my rejection of the Three Persons/Three Gods in the doctrine of the Trinity. It is my personal belief and revelation that GOD the Father is the only one GOD, and there is no other GOD than only this GOD, the Creator. His one and only Son, JESUS CHRIST, resides in Him. The Holy Spirit or Holy Ghost, the divine power, resides in GOD the Father and in Jesus Christ and works through the CROSS. Without the CROSS, it is impossible to arrive at the truth of the revelation, to meet the truth of God. In fact, the CROSS of Christ is the source of all our questions that refer to the revelation of God.

When we talk about revelation, we should put the CROSS in our Christian mind and thinking. Let us plant all Christian principles, doctrines, and convictions in the root of the heart of the Crucified Christ. The closer we approach the CROSS of Christ, the more we get bound to the Truth of GOD.

The CROSS is holy, and only by the CROSS will we arrive in God's kingdom. This revelation of God is only to be perceived in the fortitude of the CROSS. Through the CROSS, the revelation will come to us and God and Christ can speak to us. Here at the foot of the CROSS in the light of Christ's Resurrection will we experience the true existence of GOD the Father and Jesus Christ, God's only Begotten Son, who is not, I repeat, not God the Son.

I realize that this revelation contradicts the nature of Christianity. I realize as well that my position may be seen to be absurd, but truth has always been an enemy to unfounded beliefs, and as long we have faith in truth, there is nothing we need to fear The life of a true Christian should be a revelation of the eternal power and Divinity of the CRUCIFIED CHRIST.

★33 Pensees, tr. W. F. Trotter. (London: J. M. Dent & Sons, Ltd. and New York: E. P. Dutton & Co., Inc., 1932), No. 430, p.118

Literature References:

Philosophy of Religon- John Hick

Got Vater Got Sohn Und Heiliger Geist: H. Th. Lilipaly

De Grote Opdracht: H. Th. Lilipaly

A BRIEF NOTE
FROM THE AUTHOR:

This booklet is written and published with reference to the messages and revelations which I, a Christian from Indonesia, by God's mercy and through deep and constant struggle in my prayers for God's Reality and Truth, have directly received from Christ in a supernatural way.

The reader will be entering a world where over and over again the reader will be confronted directly with JESUS CHRIST and HIS CROSS.

May this booklet be a blessing to the reader and may CHRIST lead you in the truth of His Revelations.

God the Father and JESUS CHRIST bless you.

Hendrik Th. Lilipaly (1902 – 1990)

From: *De Verlosser en Rechter der mensen* (1982, Danziger Str.5k, 6301, Pohlheim 6, Germany), translated by: Andre C. Aki

Jesus Christ,
the Redeemer of Mankind

Jesus Christ, God's Son, came into this world so that through His suffering and death at the Cross, humankind could be redeemed from sin. This redemption is His Finished Work.

Jesus Christ, the Savior of the world, was born on December 28 at 9:45 P.M. and died on the Cross on Friday, April 17, at 6:47 P.M. Humankind has sinned and fallen in sin. Because of the transgression of sin that produced many injustices, humankind has rebelled totally against God. Humankind has willfully violated this principle and is therefore personally responsible to God. Humankind was confined in the halls of sin, where the inner soul decomposed, decayed, and spiritually died because of sins and misdeeds. Because of the fall, God has become an unreachable mountaintop surrounded by an immeasurable abyss. Christ came to this world to reunite fallen humankind with God, to take away the debt that is laid on humankind and to bring humankind back into Gods arms.

"For God so loved the world that He gave His only begotten Son, so that whoever believeth in Him should not perish but have everlasting life" (John 3:16). God has sent His Son to this world so that whatever He has created could be saved. From the inaccessible glory of heaven as God's throne, let us flee with our thoughts down to earth. In the fullness of time, Christ came. The Word became flesh, and through the heart of His sufferings he came into this world and lived among humankind.

The Word becoming flesh is God's mystery, which supersedes our intellect. In this instance, we should not try to literally interpret the truth and the occurrence of the Word becoming the flesh of the Lord if we do not want to arrive at conclusions that do not contain any truth. It is God's secret. The Word is the immeasurable secret of God's grace and liberty that wants to protect us. We should realize that we are able to solve the mystery of the Word becoming the flesh of the Lord only at the Cross and be aware that the mystery mainly relates to the unrestrained love of God in the Cross of His Son. If we seriously struggle with Christ's own words before and at the Crucifixion, we will understand that Christ, through the Cross, has come to us whom Christ Himself has created. Through the heart of Christ's sufferings, God's Son abandoned His heavenly paradise and came to this world.

His suffering in this world began in the manger of Bethlehem and ended at Calvary's hill when Christ proclaimed at the Cross, *IT IS FINISHED!*

Come. Let us go in spirit to Golgotha. In spirit, we are at the foot of the Cross. We bow our heads. We untie our shoes. And with our hearts we pray at the feet of God's Son, Jesus Christ.

Here we are confronted with God's holy presence, which has manifested in the Crucified One and speaks to us in the silence of the suffering of His Son. Here at the Cross we stand, breathless, in the intensity of our prayer, as our whole being is confronted with the sight of Him, the Crucified One. Here at the foot of the Cross, through God's Holy Spirit, the secret and the mystery of Golgotha will be revealed to us through our deep and steadfast prayer struggle. Definitely here will the mystery of God be revealed to those to whom Christ has chosen to reveal the mystery.

In the midst of Christ's suffering at the Cross our spirit is stirred because God's hands save us so that we may understand a small piece of the huge mystery of God, which is the Crucifixion of God's Son to save and redeem the lost sinner. The immeasurable suffering of Jesus Christ must stir in our sinners' souls the fundamental opposite of God and humankind, the majesty of God and the insignificance of humankind. These are the opposites of forgiveness and sin: the forgiving God, the sinful human being.

When the Son of God was dying on the Cross, there was complete silence at Golgotha as if it were a graveyard. Darkness invaded the entire land; yes, complete darkness surrounded the Cross like a shroud. Here in front of the Cross, in God's presence, we are standing in silent awe. His countenance makes us tremble. We hear a mothers cry echoing in the boundless night. And not one, as it is written in the Bible, but two disciples, Andrew and John, were witnessing Christ's suffering and dying.

While we listen to the cry of abandonment, *"Eloi, Eloi lama sabachtani"* ("My God, My God, why have you forsaken me?" Matthew 27:46), a stir goes down our spines. In deepest abandonment, the Son holds with one hand His Father's hand and with His other hand the sinner's hand. The brightest Light that ever shone in the world is snuffed out in the darkness.

Is this the end? No, it is not the end. A Light came. A divine, beaming light of God's heavenly bliss shines on the countenance of His Son, whose eyes are looking up to heaven.

The Son, who knows that everything is finished, speaks to His Father in the divine language, a language which neither we human beings nor even the angels can understand. The Father replies, and with a loud voice, strong and without stammering, the Lord cries out, "IT IS FINISHED" (John 19:30). That is the victory. This jubilant victory cry sounds with a blasting power that penetrates throughout the entire universe, making Lucifer and his demons tremble while the angels sing and give jubilant praise.

During Christ's Crucifixion at Golgotha (Calvary), Lucifer, the king of darkness, was present with all his demonic underworld followers. During the Crucifixion, Satan produced the blasphemy of God's Son, spoken through humans, Satan, through the people, spoke to the Lord: "If You are God's Son, redeem yourself, and come off the Cross" (Luke 23:35). Satan waited and waited. Had the Lord come off the Cross, the world would have totally, one hundred percent, fallen into Satan's hands. But Christ, God's Son, did not come off the Cross. Already, that indicated Satan's defeat. Prior to the victorious cry, "IT IS FINISHED," Satan left the stage of the Crucifixion and said, "It can't be different. Christ is God," The painful cry. *"Eloi, Eloi lama sabachtani,"* grips the sinner to the deepest depth of his or her soul.

The victory cry, "IT IS FINISHED." has made the sinner broken-heartedly, bleedingly, thankful while kneeling at the pierced feet of the Crucified One, his Redeemer and Savior. Here, at the foot of the Cross, in the Light of Christ's victory is the real Easter. After the defeat of the Cross comes the jubilant victory of His Finished Work. The response of God the Father to His Son means whatever had or had not transpired at the grave: He who died is risen to eternal life and what falls under Gods judgment has received in the Cross the legitimacy of His approval. And *not* after the Crucifixion, at the Resurrection on the third day, as has been proclaimed by theologians through the ages.

"IT IS FINISHED!" This victory cry of Christ at the Cross is the divine proclamation to the entire world, to heaven and to hell, that Jesus Christ is the Victor from Calvary. The grand redemption plan is jubilantly finished by Christ, the battle between Christ and Satan is decided, the debt is paid, and the reign of sin is defeated.

God's Son has entirely finished everything that was necessary for the redemption and deliverance of the world and eternal life for us. Christ has done it for us, but without us. The deliverance of humankind has been accomplished in the Cross. Jesus Christ is therefore in the Cross, the Redeemer of humankind. The sacrificial offering has been accomplished.

Through His Finished Work, Christ not only brings back the relationship between God and humankind but also rehabilitates the relationship of God and us, between the Creator and the created! The Cross is the center of the restoration. The Cross is the only spot where the disconcerted and broken relationship between God and man is restored honorably by Christ's offering. Only in the Cross are we truly restored people. This also means that without the Cross as the way to Christ, we can never be restored with God. We should therefore confess that the Cross is the way to Christ, to God. Without Christ, we can never reach God, and Christ cannot be reached without the Cross. To come to Christ, we must travel the way to Golgotha where the Cross is waiting for us as the only assurance in our search for the truth. Therefore, there is no other way for man to reach God than the road via Golgotha. IT IS FINISHED! This means that Jesus Christ, through His Cross, has opened the gate to God's throne and given us, who because of sin was destined to receive eternal death, eternal life. For every sinner, the Cross has opened the road to the Eternal Light, the way for a new life, the way to eternal life, the way to God's kingdom, the way to God's heart. This road exists as long as we live and die with Christ and His Cross and Resurrection, as long as we totally accept His Finished Work. Christ's triumphant cry means that the Cross rises up to the heavens, which are immeasurable and without bounds.

The Finished Work declares that Jesus Christ is the only way to come to God the Father. That is God's Truth. The truth of His Resurrection and the truth of His Kingdom. The working of His spirit is inhabited in the Cross. The final answers to all questions related to God and Jesus Christ are to be found only in the Cross. "IT IS FINSIHED!" This victory cry is the divine proclamation to all mankind that believing in the Finished Work of Christ at the Cross at Golgotha is the only key to the kingdom of God. The Cross is the key that allows us to open the gate to God's kingdom. In the light of the great Salvation and Redemption, we are victors over sin and evil power. This means that the Salvation and Redemption are the breakthrough of Christ's victory through the Cross in our lives. Salvation is for anyone who embraces Christ's Finished Work. Anyone can enjoy the fruits of this universal victory. This victory is declared to be inherent to the divine character of God's Son. This redemption and salvation are what God has prepared for the sinner and set forth in Christ's suffering and death. The sinner may take part in the resurrection of Christ. In the resurrection we should see the road that is paved by the Cross, the road to God, the road to Truth. Jesus Christ has accomplished and finished everything for us. Thanks to His Finished Work in Christ's human nature-as we used to call it-is absorbed in God, which is the contrast between the divine and the human conquered in the Cross. We are thus *in* the Cross blessed human beings, and as a tiny part of the world he essentially, in the Cross, is a constituent of the divine and eternity. He possesses the freedom to come near to God at the foot of the Cross. At the Cross, through Christ's victory, God will say "yes" to us, while prior to that He could say only "no." Christ's Finished Work in the Cross has established an event of contradiction, of victory and salvation. Christ's victory at the Cross ends the old and ancient life and causes the whole of creation to appear in a renewed form. This is the new life based on the truth of the Cross. The Cross contains the core of all that is new.

This is actually the core of the Resurrection. It is the break of dawn, the very first light, the first morning glory of a new period. A new world exists with, by, and from Christ. Through Christ's salvation, a new world has been revealed, a world with the Cross as the center, as the pivot. It is Christ's world that breaks through from the heart of His Cross and conquers every death. It is a world free from all contradictions which occur in our daily lives. It is a world of conscience based upon the only eternal truth, which is the Cross, in our lives. It is a world where God rules, where God's will is executed, and where God's thoughts are realized. This new world, the world that God changed, is a world where Christ rules through His Cross. We who live in this world exist in a permanently revolutionized status, in a continuing process of being born again in the spirit of Christ. This is the true living with Christ. If we have accepted Christ's Finished Work, if the Cross totally rules our lives and thoughts, we then live in the world of Truth, a world controlled by God's revelation. The center of that Finished Work opens a new life for the sinner, a new life of a new era and new obligations. If we live in this new world, then we should always see God's hand rescuing the deeply lost sinner from the despair in life. And then the reality of God's revelation will rise before us and we will hail and solely praise the Cross of the Lord Jesus Christ. This is the Truth that emits bright light over our lives until eternity. The actual Easter message is nothing else but the message of Christ's victory at the Cross.

Where Christ is not the center, the Cross destroys our world and changes it into a new world where Christ rules. The Cross destroys our old life and makes us new creatures longing for Him Who is the Resurrection and Life. What is taken away from us because of His righteousness is given back by His grace in the Cross. The Cross of Christ therefore means Grace.

But, unfortunately, the Cross has been treated as a truth with which people do not want to meddle. The Cross has been trampled by our so-called thinking. The Christian world with its centuries-long tradition pays only moderate attention to the profound meaning of the Cross. Christians would like to receive grace from God, but without the Cross. Do we not realize that Jesus Christ, through the Cross, with the breakthrough of His suffering and death, has reopened the Divine source of grace? Has it become somewhat clearer now to you that Jesus Christ, the Crucified One, is your Savior? Is He not the Savior and Redeemer of humankind? Is not the center of this truth the Cross of Jesus Christ?

Jesus Christ broke through and conquered the power of sin through His bitter suffering and death at the Cross. Out of love, Christ came into this world. Because of love, Christ climbed the hill of Golgotha. Due to love, Christ died for us at the Cross. In His immeasurable love, Christ took the place of the sinful humankind. He took upon Himself the sin and the consequences thereof as debt payments for us at the Cross. All of God's wrath against the sins of all humankind has been borne by Christ, in addition to the mountains of sin which have been placed between God and humankind. He has taken our sins away. Jesus Christ was crucified and died on the Cross to save forlorn and lost humankind, to save us, to save you and me. It was our sin that put Christ to death at the Cross. Yes, it was we who nailed God's Son to the Cross. The Cross revealed not only our horrifying cruelty but also the immeasurable Divine grace that forgave our sins and re-established us through the blood of the Cross. The Cross revealed Christ's victory to us. It revealed the power of Gods hand to deliver us in this world. For the Christian, the Cross means victory, the power of God's hand to deliver us in this world. For the Christian, the Cross means victory, salvation and redemption. The Cross is the assurance and reality of salvation. It is a plan of God's love. The Cross is the manifestation of God's compassion in Christ. The Cross of Christ is the sea of God's love whose waves wash us to the eternal shores to God's arms.

"Father, into thy hands, I commend My spirit" (Luke 23:46). These words were spoken by God's Son in a loud unbroken voice five minutes after the painful cry, *"Eloi, Eloi, lama sabachtani,"* which means, "I die, yet My Spirit is in the hands of My Father. My death on the Cross means My Resurrection. Because I arise, My death does not mean that I have been cast down; rather My death means a rising up. I have power to lay down My life; I have power to raise it back up."

Christ's victory at the Cross means this: With might, Christ died. By His might in the Cross, Christ has sentenced death to die. Death has been conquered with all its consequences. God showed it to us by the shaking of the earth, by the lightening from the clouds and the rolling of the thunder. Yes, through all the events that took place during the Crucifixion and at the Resurrection on the third day, Jesus Christ was crucified, died, and rose again. He is truly God's Son, and like His Father is truly and really God.

"IT IS FINISHED!" The voice of the Savior of the World echoes through the ages, telling what happened at Golgotha. This sign lives on until today and into the future. Golgotha is the spot and the moment where eternity and the temporary meet with the victory of Christ at the Cross, the victory which shows us the mind-boggling abyss of our sinful status. With Christ Finished Work, all of our human paradigms and learning principles are overpowered and overset. Jesus Christ has finished everything which had been required for us at the Cross. Golgotha's victory cry, "IT IS FINISHED," has sounded and will sound through all the ages. It preaches to the world that only Jesus Christ, God's only begotten Son, can give bliss and contentment to humankind. This music means the breakthrough and revolution of God's Grace sprouts from the Crucified One to our hearts! Should this song be replaced by the traditional Christian symphony, which is full of dissonance? Or perhaps replaced by preaching the Gospel of Jesus Christ without penetrating into the heart of the Gospel?

We think to be able to redeem ourselves through cultural or mystical religion. We strive to live morally to perfection and think that the salvation of ourselves is our own product. We search for something we can hold on to, but on our own, without Christ. We live passionately, thinking of our religious convictions based on theological insight. And, depending on physical stimuli, we dive into the depths of uncertainty, which is never by itself explainable. We attempt by our own might to free ourselves from demonical power and expect that all human efforts can set themselves free from the suffering and pain of life. We feel as if we are happy, but in fact we are shining in a quasi-virtual happiness like a star in the midst of the blackness of the night.

Let me ask you another relevant question. Have we Christians really understood that mighty Finished Work of Christ at the Cross? Have we ever seriously understood what God's love really means? Can we imagine the length, width, and depth of God's love? Do we really realize the depths of suffering from which we have been saved by Christ? Who can give us the solution to all our problems in this life? Can we free ourselves from by our own will from sin and release ourselves from the bondage of Satan? Have we ever truly struggled with the truth of the Cross? Does the inner meaning of Christ's Cross ever come into our mind? Whosoever can provide us with a definite answer to all these questions? My answer reads: find it by no man, find it only in Jesus Christ. He alone can give us the answer to all our questions in life. Only He can give us the solution to all our problems. Only He can redeem us from the bondage of sin and set us free from evil. Because Christ Himself is the answer, Christ Himself is the solution. Christ Himself is the Redeemer, the Savior of humankind. He shall give us the answer; He will give us the solution. He will release us through His Cross by His suffering and death at Golgotha.

The Cross is placed in the center of the world, in the midst of our relationship, as the grand solution and the sign of victory. He who lives and dies with Christ, does not build on his own strength, his own biblical, philosophical principles. Christ will give him the power to hold on in his life and his struggle with the truth. From Christ, from his Finished Work, will humankind gain daily his or her strength. You will experience this strength as an ever renewing power in your life, every day, every hour of the day, in whatever circumstance. So will your life be, a life originated from the Crucified Christ, who is the Resurrection. The Cross is for humankind, the never ending source of strength, power and authority. The Cross is our anchor to hold on, to calmly stand in the midst of the storm of life. Whoever in the fight and struggle for the truth put his or her eyes on the Cross, never will he or she lose the victory. Nothing will frighten him or her whatever Satan is able to do. Except therefore Christ's Finished Work, live for Christ, suffer for Christ, fight for Christ so that your whole life becomes a devotional offering for His glory. Glorify the Cross of Christ; praise His Finished Work. Because of that grand redemption and salvation, we sinners are allowed to enter God's Kingdom. With that, God hereby requires that we confess Christ and His Cross as a living reality in and over our lives.

Dear reader, have you ever been there in the blackness of Gethsemane and in the midst in the agony of Golgotha? Look upward at the Crucified Son of God, at the condemned Cross of Golgotha, nailed for the whole of humankind. See with sublime awe the light of his sufferings covering our sight and pray that the light of His Finished Work will not strike us with eternal blindness. See the Crucified in the light of his resurrection. Listen to the voice of He who directly created the world and humankind. Listen to His voice, to Jesus Christ, God's Son. He is eternal, almighty, all knowing, and all wise and true, holy and just. Let us kneel down, with bitter tears in our eyes, at his pierced feet. The blood of Christ that is our salvation and the forgiveness of our sins. What a privilege for us Christians to know without a doubt that our salvation and redemption lie only in the Cross. Keep this in mind: what the Cross means to us and what Christ has accomplished for us. It is real joy for the soul if we always focus our sight on the Cross and realize how the Crucified Son of God, in his unending grace has come down to this world from heavens glory to Golgotha's mind boggling agony, pain and suffering for our salvation. Should not we therefore thank God the Father and His Son? Yes, glorify and praise them in this life until it is time for us to die. Listen now to the voice of Jesus Christ resounding into this world in the midst of all suffering and need, through all things and ages: "Sinner, believe, accept My Finished Work. Pray with all your heart and soul to understand My sufferings and death. If you decide not to confess the Cross as a living reality in your life, then you are the murderer of your own soul. I am giving you the very last chance. Make a decision right now. Do not wait until tomorrow. I await your decision"

If you have seriously struggled and remain struggling with the truth of the Cross, I hope the following principles will not fall on deaf ears:

The Cross of Jesus Christ is the highest revelation of God's love, where Christ has reconciled humankind with God. Christ in the Cross reconciled an act as the only true Son of God.

Christ's Cross - which is God's judgment but at the same time also means the nullification of the judgment is the salvation of humankind.

The Cross set us free from the bondage of death: it raised us up in the light of Gods kingdom.

The Cross of Christ is the point where our souls can enjoy God's love, away from pain and suffering, free from agony, and our eyes can see the majesty of God the Father in the light of Christ's Finished Work.

The core of the Cross is an endless ocean of which the width and depth totally and absolutely is immeasurable.

The Cross comprises an unending divine power and reflects thereby God's universal reality and love in Christ.

The Cross points humankind to a deeper meaning regarding Christ. The Cross leads the Christian, through biblical interpretation to discover new areas within the boundaries of God's Truth and revelation.

The Cross of Jesus Christ presents solid ground for humankind to stand so that humankind is secure, however stormy and rough the sea may be.

The Cross of Jesus Christ, the Savior and Redeemer of humankind presents to us life that remains to the end in time of suffering, in the battle, in the storm, in the night until death.

May the Cross of Jesus Christ lead you and me to God's eternal truth.

Jesus Christ –
the Judge of Mankind

God is the Father of Jesus Christ. Nobody knows who the Son is except the Father, and who the Father is except the Son, and those to whom the Son wishes to reveal. Jesus Christ reveals the Divine mysteries only in accordance with His Divine decision. According to the Divine mysteries and only in accordance to His Divine decision, according to the Divine plan, these ages-old, ready made Divine secrets are, by order of Jesus Himself, being revealed to those to whom Christ wants to reveal them.

Because of His Finished Work at the Cross, all power and authority are given to Christ in heaven and on earth. Jesus Christ is, in the Cross, the direct Creator and Savior of mankind. All activities and performances of Christ at the time of creation as well as at the redemption have been totally blended together to become His power and strength as the Son of God.

Jesus Christ was crucified, died, arose, and ascended to God His Father. Prior to Christ's ascension, God spoke through the Angel Gabriel and instructed all the angels to arrange for the heavenly celebration of Christ's glorious homecoming and His inauguration to the Throne.

The Angel Gabriel prepares himself as the trumpeter. The trumpeter is beginning to sound his trumpet. The flags are being raised, the bells are ringing, the sounds of the heavenly gongs and anvils vibrate through the heavens, penetrating all the heavenly spheres.

For the second time, the Angel blows the trumpet. The sound merges with the music of angelic choirs. Surrounded by heavenly celestials, Christ, God's Son, makes His entrance into heaven. The name CHRIST creates music on the heavenly harps, music in mighty chords of praise and joy that fills the heavens. The heavenly celestials parade through the heavenly tracks.

The jubilant praise of angels vibrates through the heavens. The angelic choir echoes softly against the waves of the heavenly oceans and joins the music of golden harps. For the very first time since the creation, a parade is being held in the heavens. Under the jubilant praise of angels and those blessed in Christ, Jesus Christ is installed with honor and glory on His Father's supreme throne.

The trumpet resounds for the third time and with a powerful voice, the Angel proclaims, *May God and Jesus Christ, the direct creator of the whole universe, the Redeemer and Savior of mankind, be praised and glorified for all eternity. Glory to God, glory to Jesus Christ, our direct Creator, the Almighty Son of God. Adore Him. Obey Him in every aspect and do whatsoever He commands us to do. Adore and hail Him who has created the heavens and the earth and the sea and the water wells. Be always ready for the battle. If He commands, descend like lightning and thunder to the earth. Assist the true believers in Christ; assist God elect' in their battle for the truth and in their battle against the demonic power, Satan, the devil, and his entire demonic kingdom.*

Jesus Christ is now sitting on the throne in heaven, far above all earthly authority and power and dominion. He rules and controls this world with the tools of His power, with His grace and wisdom. His scepter reaches out to all things, to all angels and people. Through Christ, God opens all aspects to govern all things in the heavens and on earth. All things are subject to Him. Guided by His might and justice under His Divine existence. Christ rules and governs the world according to His Divine will. This power of Christ has no limits. Like His Father, Christ possesses the ultimate sovereignty. This sovereignty manifests itself completely in His suffering and death, in His Finished Work on the Cross at Golgotha.

Appointment of the Angel Gabriel

Based on the divine revelation to me, we may know that after the fall of Lucifer, the head of the fallen angels, Jesus Christ temporarily appointed the Angel Gabriel to be the head of all angels. After Christ's inauguration, the Angel Gabriel was definitely appointed as the head of all angels. (August 22 is the day of the Angel Gabriel.) This angel is directly subservient to Jesus Christ and possesses the most knowledge about God and His works. All messages, revelations, commands, and God's decisions, yes, everything that is passed personally, either through Gabriel or through other angels to the blessed souls on earth, everything is given by direct order of Christ. All other angels are obliged to listen to Gabriel and required to carry out his orders. As head of all angels, the Angel Gabriel has two representatives (De Grote Opdracht, John's Uitgeverij, Heerlen, Netherlands, 1973 p. 79), both of whom have been given new names, Korinsien and Nansirien, by God the Father and Christ.

Christ has given authority to the Angel Gabriel to punish the world with earthquakes, floods, fires, typhoons, and other "acts of God." The angel knows no mercy because his sword, which drove Adam and Eve out of paradise, knows no mercy. In addition to his appointment of the Angel Gabriel, Christ has appointed, in accordance to His Divine decision through all ages, one of the chosen messengers of God to be the head of all messengers of God for a temporary period (the heavenly period). All of God's messengers, the chosen as well as the unchosen, must obey His orders. All divine decisions are related to the tasks and assignments of people in this world who are specially assigned to God's plan.

Jesus Christ is the Judge of the world, the Judge of humankind. After the appointment of the Angel Gabriel as head of all angels came Christ's decision to mark the Books of Faith (degree of faith) and Books of Good and Evil. These books, which are mentioned in John's revelation, are being scrutinized by hundreds of angels. Christ is the rightful Judge of the living and the dead. He judges and passes judgment on humanity based on what was written and noted in those books and in the Book of Life. Everything takes place in accordance to His Divine measure, the measure of His holy Cross, the one and only never-failing barometer.

Christ is the God of judgment and Mercy. Christ is the Lawgiver and the Judge. He has the power to save and to destroy. He executes the law from the spirit of His Finished Work on the Cross at Golgotha. God the Father does not pass judgment on anyone, but has given the entire judgment to His Son, Jesus Christ. Christ exercises judgment, passes sentence, and redeems us through the Cross. How we Christians stand before Christ and His Cross, what level of faith we reach at the time of our death, and what our actions were on earth-these things are for Christ to decide our eternal fate. All of our actions on earth and our faith and belief in God will be revealed at Christ's holy Judgment Seat. Jesus Christ, the Judge, knows all of our secrets. Christ is the Perceiver of our hearts. He explores our hearts. He knows our lives. He sees all our deeds. He hears the words we speak. He reads the deepest secret depths of our souls. Not one creature can hide from Him because all of our faith in Christ, because our actions, ideas, thoughts, and desires, both good and evil, are all in the open and lie naked in front of Christ. We are accountable. We will be judged.

Christ's decision is the divine decision, the decision of God. Based on His Finished Deliverance and Redemption at Golgotha, the forgiveness of sin is granted directly by Jesus Christ Himself. Only the Second Coming of Christ, when Christ appears on the clouds of heaven in glittering glory and majesty, only when Christ returns surrounded by legions of celestial beings on the last Judgment Day, will God the Father determine the preference. Christ's requirements for us to enter God's kingdom have become tougher these days. No one in the world can enter God's kingdom without Christ's Holy Cross. Christ's Cross is holy because it is the key to the kingdom of God. Because of Christ's Deliverance and Redemption at the Cross, the following divine decision has been declared:

God's kingdom belongs only to those who belong to Christ's Cross. God kingdom demands that we live in the Cross. To live in the Cross means to be within Christ. Only in the Cross can we meet the real Christ. To believe in the Finished work of Christ at the Cross should be the main theme of our religion.

The Cross is the way to Christ, the path to God, the road to God's kingdom. The truth of the Cross should become the dominating, living element of our faith and our belief. The Cross is the result of Christ's work that bums and blazes personal faith in the heart of every Christian and established the mystical unity of individual human beings with Christ and with God the Father.

God asks us,

What is your standpoint at this present moment, you, Christian, who name yourself to Christ, in regard to the reality of Christ and His Cross? What is your stance towards His Finished work? Do you search for Christ in His Cross? Does Christ, the Victor from Golgotha, rule your life and thoughts? Have you ever knelt with tears of regret at the foot of the Cross, feeling that you were the greatest sinner on earth? Are you fighting for the truth?

The Christian is being put to the test by the reality of the Cross. Are we Christians directing our knowledge, wisdom, thoughts, and ideas to the manifestation of the Cross as God's highest revelation? Or are we attempting to use our own intellect without the Cross? As the light reveals itself in darkness, so does the Cross to the Christian. The Cross is the testing ground for our belief and faith in Christ, whatever we claim our spiritual conviction to be, whether it is real or unreal. The Cross is Christ's Light and remains in the world as the Light of Christ out of God's Light. The Cross is the one and only key to God's mystery. The belief in the Cross by the undertaking of Christ's spirit brings forth the living reality, the actuality of God's being.

Golgotha will create a split in humankind. We will form into two groups. The first group will consist of those who realize their natural situation and admit that as a result of their sins, they are doomed and are bound for destruction. The other group, unfortunately, the majority, consists of those who are ignorantly looking at the Cross of Christ while they are blinded by their sins and tossed around in the dark and hardening their hearts to God.

They seldom look at the Cross because their activities, desires, and enjoyments have filled up their lives. They ignore the salvation offered by Christ and remain under God's curse.

Many Christians claim God's grace and love based on the words of the apostles in 1 John 2:1, Romans 8:26, 27, 34, and Hebrews 7:25, which reads as follows: *But if anyone does sin, we have Jesus Christ the righteous who pleads for us with the Father. The spirit himself pleads with God for us.* Jesus Christ pleads with God for us to save those who come to God through Him, because He lives forever to plead with God for them.

Do not these interpretations of Bible texts create confusion in our thinking? Should we not read and understand them in the light of the Truth? We must read those Biblical texts in the light of the Cross, which means in the light of the Crucified One Who is The Truth.

Jesus Christ is not a plea bargainer. He does not plead with God the Father for us. The spirit, the Holy Spirit, the spirit of Christ, does not plead for us to God the Father, nor does the spirit of God plead to God. Jesus Christ the Judge judges and passes sentence on us. To Him, God the Father has passed the entire Judgment. Christ has the power and is authorized to determine judgment. But now we ask,

Is this not what has been preached about God, Christ and the Holy Spirit? Is it a piling up of one meaning upon another so that the two refute each other? Don't we feel that our brains have become graveyards stuffed with conclusions that are not based on truth? Can we confidently know who God is and who Jesus Christ truly is without a direct revelation, a revelation straight from the Absolute and Eternal from whence creation was brought into existence?

The Judgment
of the Divine Judge

I speak with conviction. Christ is the just Judge Who is guided by truth. He judges and passes judgment based on what is declared in the Books of Faith, in the Books of Good and Evil, and in the Book of Life. All judgments take place in accordance to His divine measurement. It is our human destiny to die one day and face judgment. Christ passes judgment over us.

His judgment begins at the time of our death. Right after we die, Jesus Christ the Judge renders His decision as whether we go directly to heaven or to the dark continents of tears and the gnashing of teeth. And if we have not yet met the standard placed by Christ and are not able to enter God's kingdom because our faith has not met the minimum standard, our soul goes to the place of indecision, or our life is spared and extended by a couple of hours. In this instance, when we come to rest in the place of indecision, the angels appointed by Christ will visit us and preach about Jesus Christ, His Cross, and His Finished Work.

When the angels leave, the devils get their turn and preach the enjoyment of their dark continents, which to them are also called "heaven." They promise us mountains of gold. Whoever meets the requirements set by the king of darkness, to him or her will be awarded an iron crown. He or she will occupy a high position in Satan's kingdom. But not one of the devils will tell us about the torture of Satan's followers who do not follow Satan's wishes.

At the time determined by Christ, the winnowing takes place. We who meet the requirements will step into heaven and be welcomed and greeted in God's Glory. We will begin our glorious everlasting relationship with God. But we who do not meet those requirements will be thrown into the darkest, most extreme night, the night of suffering, pain and agony of God's wrath. Many who have departed from the place of indecision and arrived at the headquarters of Lucifer and his followers rebel against the Judge's decision. But His decision is firm and not likely to change. Christ's judgment is just and rightful.

If Christ decides to extend the life of the dying person by a few hours, angels will come and preach to us. They point us to Christ, His Cross, and his Finished Work. If, through the influence of God's spirit, our faith rises and we meet the minimum faith requirement, then we will leave this world full of tears and our souls will be escorted by guiding angels and God's messengers up to heaven, the place of eternal music and radiant white robes.

We are doomed to die. We must accept and acknowledge Christ's Cross and His Finished Work. The only chance to escape condemnation is through the Cross of Jesus Christ. The Cross is waiting for us in order to save us. The Cross calls on us with this appeal: *Be at peace with God, accept Christ's Finished Work at Golgotha, and confess the Cross as a living reality in life and living and dying with Christ is the entry to heaven.* If we reject the Cross or recognize it only as a historical artifact, then we are doomed to hell. We, who reject the Cross, reject Christ, reject God, and reject life. We are cursed and doomed. Christ will appear as the Judge; we cannot escape from Him.

We should know the following. Not by being baptized, not by being a church member, a member of a sect, a member of any organization, not by being anointed by one or more gifts of the Spirit, not even if we think we have been saved, truly inspired, and baptized by the Holy Ghost–not by any of these things will we be set free by the heavenly judgment seat. We will be proclaimed free only if we confess Christ and His Cross as a living reality in our lives. If without stopping, we remorsefully kneel down every day at the foot of the Cross and confess to being the greatest sinner on earth and in our daily lives, only then will we know the one truth of God, namely: Jesus Christ and Him Crucified.

Jesus Christ and His Cross are inseparable. This is the Divine Truth. We have free will. We are not forced to accept this truth. Consequently, if we don't want to accept this reality, there can be no spot in our heart for Christ. We will then rush unavoidably into the darkness of life, into the darkness of religious doubt, where we will meet the devil. The devil will persevere to conquer our spiritual vision and possess us entirely. Without Christ and His Cross, everything in this world is only touching the darkness like a moth flying to the flame of destruction.

Without Christ and His Cross, we will definitely die in our sins. We will be where God is not. We have created for ourselves a hell. We will not be released from God's wrath by believing that Christ's death is enough. We can be saved only through accepting Christ's Cross as our faith.

We must make the Cross our haven. If the Cross of Christ is not within our sight, our soul is dead because of our sins. If our soul is dead, it cannot enter the heavenly kingdom. We then will taste the bitterness of God's wrath. Rejected by Christ's judgment, we will surely come in revolt because we believe that God is so merciful. But Jesus Christ is not only merciful and loving, but also just and righteous.

Christ the Judge of the world is sending warnings to humankind. He punishes those who do not know God and are ignorant of the Cross, which is the source of God's grace and love. Christ is angered by our sins. Christ's indignation at our sins is like a burning flame. He punishes with the rod of His burning rage. He ordered the Angel Gabriel to use the rod and let it fall upon us so that Christians may come to truthful repentance. This repentance is a daily, continual, unending repentance which cumulates in a total and absolute change in our life and thoughts.

In spite of everything, God's love is still burning to save us from destruction. Has not the situation in the world in the last years given us an indication of God's wrath? This is the wrath which can destroy us entirely. Do we not realize this? Has it not been revealed to us that the powers of darkness are on the offensive? Numerous God-believing people have fallen into Satan's claws, which will sweep them to the abyss of darkness. This old world will vanish. Before Christ banishes the world, however, He makes us understand the suffering and pain of the disasters that are hanging above our heads. Disasters will soon strike the world, calamities that have never before taken place, not since the beginning of the world. Extreme hostility, hatred, and anger of men for their neighbors will release powers that can destroy the world. These are powers that we, no matter how scientific we think we are, can never imagine.

I was once asked if Christ is also the judge of angels. Yes, I replied. Based on a divine revelation, I may pass on the following:

On Tuesday, September 28, 1948, at 12 midnight (earth time), a meeting of selected angels and God's messengers, headed by the Head of all angels, was convened. A decision was to be made regarding where to announce God's decisions. The decision was made, but one of the angels was not in total agreement with the decision of Christ. As a consequence this angel was banished from heaven and sent to the kingdom of Lucifer, prince of darkness. The angel's name was L.

Through this divine decision, Christ reveals that He also is the judge of angels. God the Father has delegated all power and authority to Christ in heaven and on earth. This needs to be said again and again.

What I have revealed about Jesus Christ, the judge of humankind is God's mystery. By God's grace, it was revealed to me on Wednesday. August 31,1966. It is difficult for Christians to accept my revelations. Why is this so? For three reasons:

1. Most people declare that personal revelation is not referenced in the Holy Book. Most of us use the Bible as our sole source of information and base revelation only on John's revelation, Rev. 22:18, 19. We consider the Bible to be the encyclopedia of all God's mysteries.

2. Most people tend to oppose anything that goes against the old, rooted, traditional beliefs. We see these as long established absolutes, even though we do not have the certainty as whether these come from the Spirit of Truth.

3. Most people will accept only evidence which we can check with our senses or confirm with rational thought.

To those who are skeptical with regard to the mysteries of the heavens, I put forth this question:

Don't you believe that there are blessed ones in the twentieth century whose visual and mental perceptions are lightened by Christ so that they can sense and perceive a vision given by the heavenly kingdom? That there are some people given the privilege to see and hear something of that kingdom?

For the blessed souls who receive personal revelation from heaven, what they experience is too powerful to adequately describe in normal human language. Based on their revelations and according to God's grace, they may, however, pass their revelations on to others. God does not ask if we are in agreement with His actions. Jesus Christ reveals God's mysteries only to those whom He wishes.

Should we not be eternally thankful for the highest revelation of God, which is the Cross of Jesus Christ? Should we not thank God from the bottom of our hearts for this special grace given to us now in these times, in a century full of troubles, questions, and theological confusion?

THE VOICE OF
ETERNAL JUDGMENT

The voice of the Judge, the voice of the Final Judgment speaks to us before it is too late:

What do you think of the Cross of Jesus Christ?

Based on our response, we will know ourselves. Our answer will determine our ultimate destiny, which will be either the eternal light, in which we can view God's supreme bliss in complete happiness and contentment to be with God the Father and the Son of God, or the everlasting darkness of complete separation from God and Christ. If this becomes our destiny, then we will hear the final judgment: You are doomed in hell. What an anguished judgment this is. A shuddering fear goes through our bones that this judgment will justly be made upon all who do not confess and accept Christ and His Cross, including His Finished Work and Resurrection, as a living reality in their lives. In the deepest depth of their souls these words will resound: *Eternal darkness, hide us from the Judge's sight.*

DEAR READER,

Take flight today to the Cross of Jesus Christ. Run to Him, the Crucified One, before it is too late and your poor soul is judged. We don't know how our life will be tomorrow. We are a drop of dew that glistens for a moment and then vanishes. Some of us will have a long life, while others will have a short one. Some of us already have one foot in the grave. What if Judgment Day brings the curtain down now? Beware that even a just and fair man or woman can barely be saved.

Spend some time daily in the environment of Golgotha. In silence, shed thankful tears to Him, Who through His suffering and death and through His Finished Work at the Cross, has reunited you with God. To you will then be extended the invitation to enter the eternal kingdom of our Lord and Savior Jesus Christ. You then can listen to the glorious angelic choir and to the words of God's messengers in admiration and praise to their Creator. It is a song that swells in volumes and harmony and shouts down our brief, transient human passions.

Give thanks to God for the Cross of His Son. We think that our thoughts are focused on the living Christ, but without the Cross as our center, this is deceptive and false. Thank Christ for His Cross, for His Finished Work. Is not Christ the rock of your soul? Praise and glorify the name of Jesus Christ, Thank God for Golgotha's victory cry, IT IS FINISHED!

That victory cry will never cease because it is His cry that through His Cross that He has conquered the world. Jesus Christ is the same, yesterday, today, tomorrow, and for eternity. He is the direct Creator, the Savior, and the Judge of mankind.

Is Every
Message from God?

The power of God's love enables us to understand messages and revelations. By order of Jesus Christ, the angels deliver God's messages and decisions to those elect or blessed souls who were given a special task in His divine plan. The appearance of angels marks the penetration of God's light in the darkness of this world. After the messages have been delivered, the angels return to Heaven in the glory of the Eternal Light, leaving the elect, or blessed, soul to struggle at the foot of the Cross with those messages, which create a revolution in our way of thinking. Christ works in the elect through the Cross. The Cross also destroys in the elect every nature of conceited appearance and importance and the Cross changes our weakness into strength.

The elect, or blessed~souls also need to know that we are powerless against the power of darkness. For many years, I struggled to find the truth until Christ showed me His Cross. Christ has given me a task to accomplish. Satan and many people will be against me. God does not ask us to approve His actions. God, Jesus Christ, reveals Himself only to those whom He chooses. Since we no longer live in the world of the Old Testament, but in that of the New Testament (in other words, in the era after the Crucifixion of Christ), Christ now and only now reveals Himself in the Cross. Through the Cross, Christ reveals many mysteries of God.

In the first years of my struggle with the problem of God and Christ, Satan appeared to me in the form of an angel. In the midst of those temptations, I found Christ's Cross. After all of Satan's many temptations and cruel and devilish attempts to lure me away from God, God has finally made an end to it so that I can uninterruptedly receive His revelations. What steps I took under Christ's orders can only be known by those who in their personal struggles with the truth of the Crucified One completely realize that our lives depend totally on God's revelations in the Cross. All the attempts by the king of darkness directed at me were in concurrence with God's decision. These attempts showed me the cruel reality and power of Satan. At the same time, during these fights with the demonic power, I experienced the strength of the Cross. Those who possess this strength will never retreat.

The Cross (our only weapon for the truth) gives us this assurance: *Our victory is in Christ's victory at the Cross, in Christ's jubilant victory cry,* "IT IS FINISHED!"

I understand that many people are skeptical about angelic messages and revelations. Too many people have professed to have received revelations from God or have had heavenly dreams. Many supernatural appearances are being lightly explained as "divine revelations" or are felt to be inspired by the Holy Ghost. We have assured ourselves that we have heard voices or spoken "in tongues." From my own experience, I can say that these supernatural appearances, visions, dreams, and voices are generally from the devil, who, depending of the level of our faith, can easily influence us. Again and again, we need to ask this one question: *Is Jesus Christ, the Crucified One from Golgotha, the center of these messages?* We need to know that Satan can make us believe that he is an angel of light. It is his pleasure to misguide us and tell us of the heavenly bliss. He can also tell us of our family members who are walking on the heavenly riverbanks of God's city.

Without Christ's Cross, we will be misguided on the road of life. Without the Cross, we will end up on the wrong path. Without the Cross, we are victims of the power of the devil. We have to struggle with the truth of every revelation and message. We should not hold on to Biblical texts (such as John 22:18-19) and reject other revelations as *scharmerei,* or nonsense. Every message needs to be viewed in the light of the Crucified One. Each message is truly from God when it refers only to God, to Jesus Christ and His Cross. Every message or revelation should point us to God's revelation in the Cross to Christ, the Crucified One Who is the Risen One.

I realize that readers will read my words with prejudice and defend their traditional beliefs. But what we need to do is defend only the truth. The Cross should be our only weapon in our fight for the truth. The Cross is the assurance of the truth. To be more precise, the Cross leads us *directly* to Christ, if we have Christ, then we have the truth. This is the assurance. The Cross is therefore the assurance of the truth. It is going to be very difficult for anyone who is bound to the traditions to change unless Christ speaks to him/her and works in him/her. Humankind can doubt.

To the readers of my books and booklets, I sincerely ask you to pray and struggle with what you read. Pray to God for wisdom and guidance so that Christ may work in you. Pray so that you may understand Jesus Christ, His Cross, His Resurrection, and His Finished Work.

We need to be careful with our judgment, because one day we all will be called and judged by God. Does not Christ pass judgment upon you and me? Christ judges according to His divine measure, which is the measure or barometer of His Holy Cross. We wish to place every message in the light of the Cross, which is the light of the Crucified One. The Crucified One is the risen Christ and He Himself will then tell us which messages are truly from God.

I have written this booklet because I believe that what has been revealed to me is true and because you, the reader, have the right to know what is revealed. For the conventional Christian, my words have the potential for enlightenment, but they may also cause some harm. The nonbeliever, the agnostic, and the so-called scientist may find my writing to be nonsense, or even evil. I apologize if this booklet has caused you to doubt, but if I don't tell you what I know and believe, then I have made myself sinful. Let me also warn you that you should not take anything I have written here as the last word. Struggle with it and read other books I have written (some were printed in Germany and the Netherlands) before you come to a conclusion.

Do not judge, or you too will be judged. For in the way that you judge others, you will be judged, and with the same measure you use, it will be measured to you (Matthew 7:1-2).